Kim has a cat. Jim has a dog.

But Viv has an odd pet.

It is a zog! Not a cat, not a dog, but a zog!

The zog is fat. It has ten red legs.

It can run and hop.

It can sit and beg.

The zog has lots of eggs!

The zog sits on the eggs.
It sits and sits.

Tap, tap, tap!
Tap, tap, tap!

Lots of zogs!

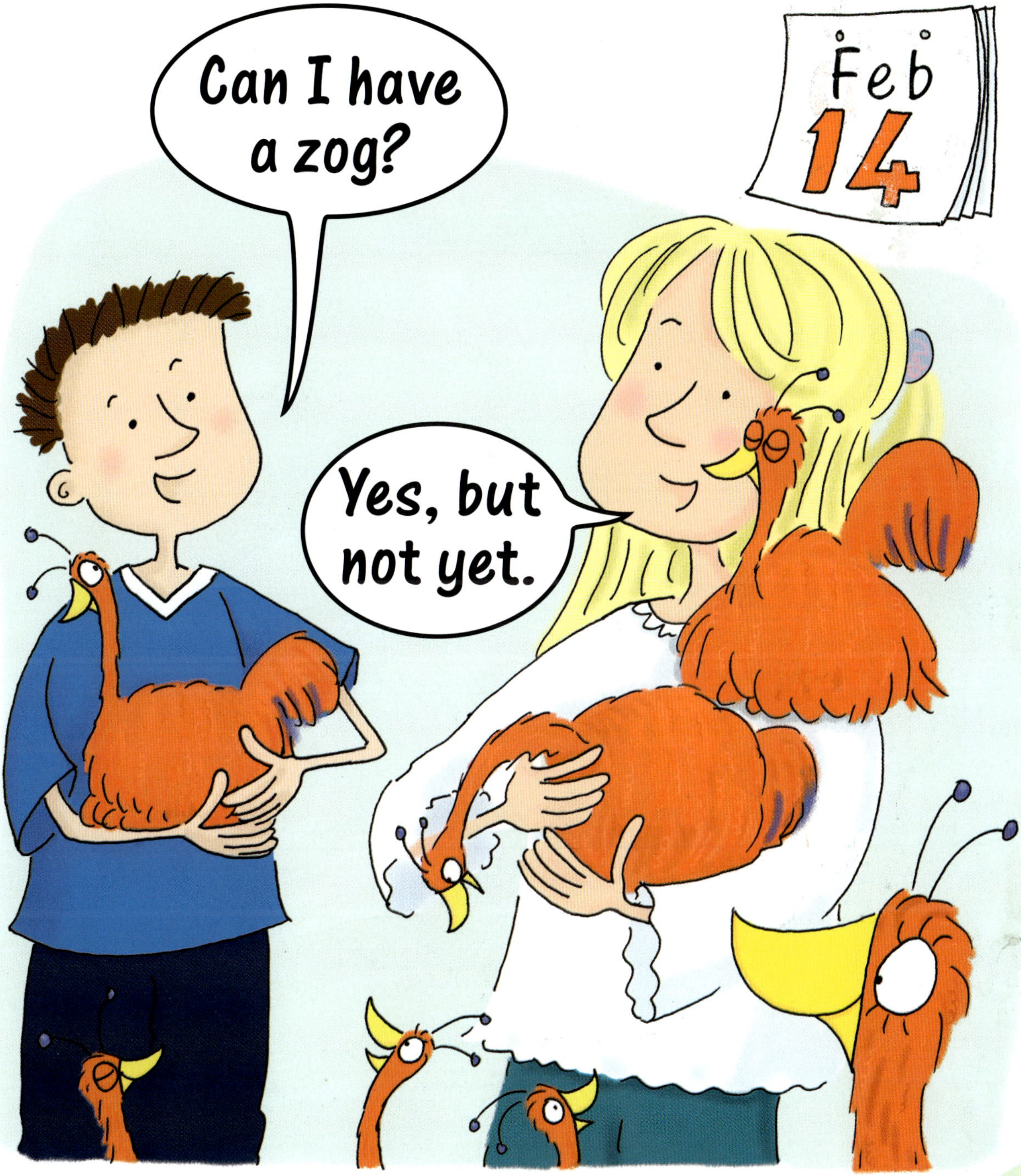
Feb 14
Can I have a zog?
Yes, but not yet.

Now Kim has a cat and a zog.

Jim has a dog and a zog.

Feb 28

And Viv has ten zogs!